Thought Patterns

Art & Poetry

Lori Arbel

ARTIST, TEACHER, CREATIVE COACH

DEDICATION

This book is dedicated to our inner light. May it be used for peace, conscientiousness, and humanitarianism.

Thank you
Ancestors
Art Masters
Mentors
Family
Creativity
&
Passion

Copyright © 2019 Lori Arbel
All rights reserved.
www.loriarbel.com

ISBN: 9781651086605

Thought Patterns explores the inner psyche including the monotonous tasks of everyday life. Using marks and a reduced, neutral palette, the artist delves into this process to question how we connect, respond, and make our mark on the world. Arbel uses introspection for content; her art making as a language. This transcendent body of work points to something beyond itself and the one who made it. It hints at the hidden story, creating a new conversation with each viewer, allowing them to explore, experience, and engage in self-discovery. Arbel is an advocate for art as a tool for positive mental health.

Pen and ink lines, handmade paper, and geometric shapes allow Arbel to express depth, texture, and pattern that result in visually energetic and meditative renderings. The imperfections of the handmade paper and pop of gold illustrate metaphor, transforming sometimes negative energy into something beautiful. Her method of working is active. She places paper on a table so that she can manoeuvre around it from all sides. In this way, Arbel can consider composition and balance from multiple perspectives while being physically engaged with her intuitive process.

CONTENTS

Order	Pg 1	Chakra Web	Pg 27
Intersection	Pg 3	Confetti	Pg 29
Breakthrough	Pg 5	Cosmic Circles	Pg 31
Deconstruction Reconstruction	Pg 7	Spiraling in Control	Pg 33
Circles & Triangles	Pg 9	Jet Stream	Pg 35
Direction	Pg 11	Synapses	Pg 37
Golden Angle	Pg 13	Phases	Pg 39
Golden Angles	Pg 15	Road Signs	Pg 41
Golden Triangle	Pg 17	Glimmers of Light	Pg 43
Happy	Pg 19	Celestial Ladders	Pg 45
Notes & Keys	Pg 21	Marks for Their Lives: 3,113	Pg 47
Wheels in Motion	Pg 23	Marks for Their Lives: 1,158	Pg 49
Aligned	Pg 25		

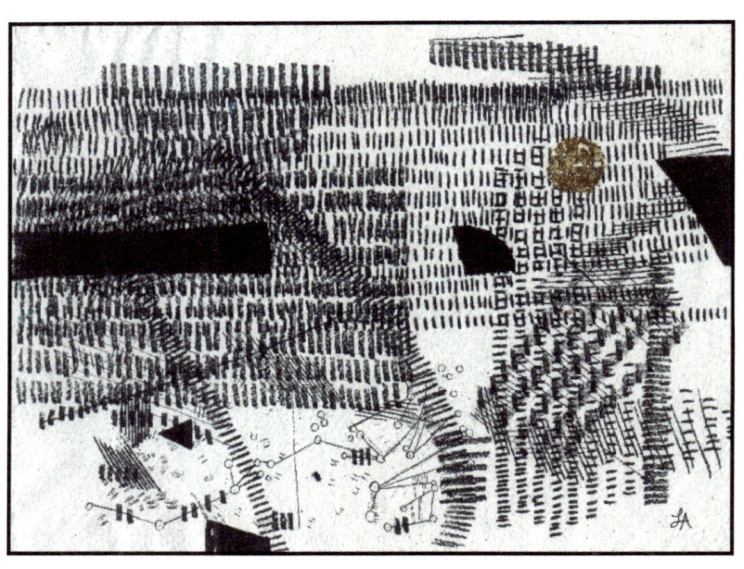

Order

Controlled chaos
Parallel lines, parallel lives
Accounted for, forgotten
Numbers, hair pulling, marks
Holocaust
Communism
Emptiness
Loss

Numbers not individuals
Side by side.

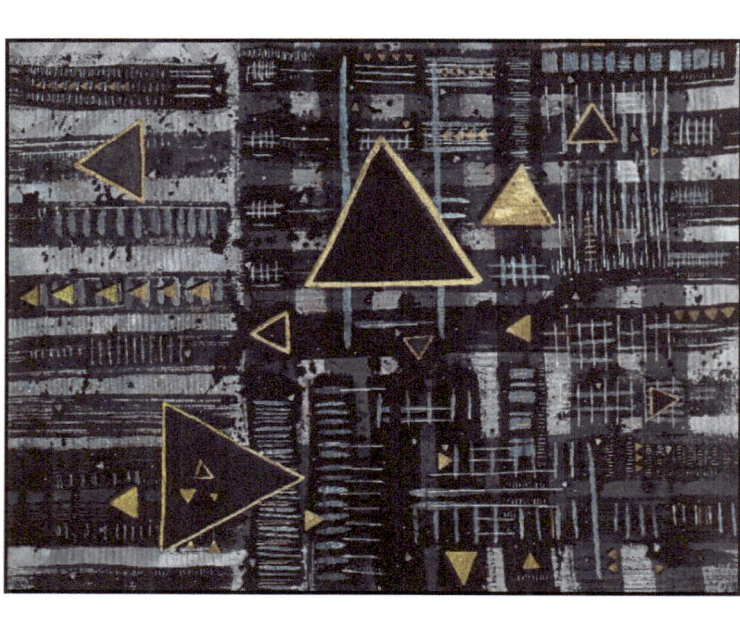

Intersection

Left, right, straight, up
In, out
Lines leading to a place
The place
Guidance, focus
Which way should I go?

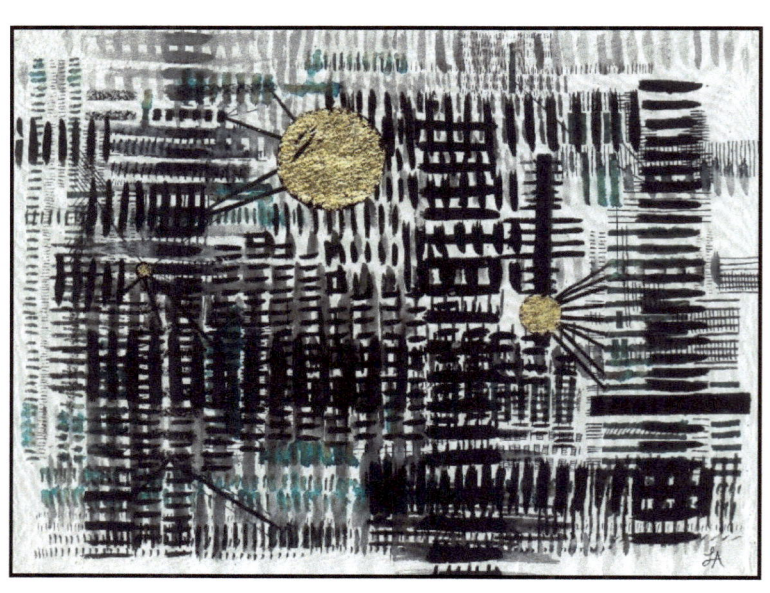

Breakthrough

Yes!
A vision beyond the vision
Dreams a reality

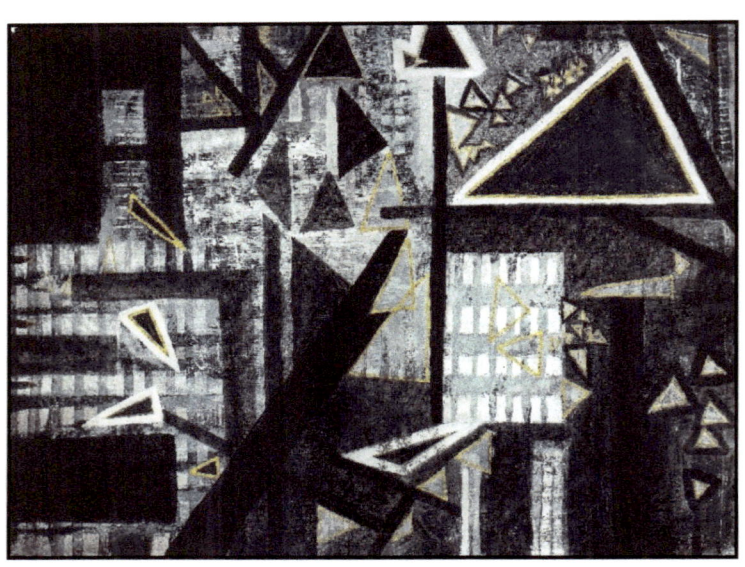

Deconstruction
Reconstruction

Process, creation
Seconds, minutes, steps;
Step back,
Disappointment,
Awe,
Go back,
Rebuild, remake, reflect

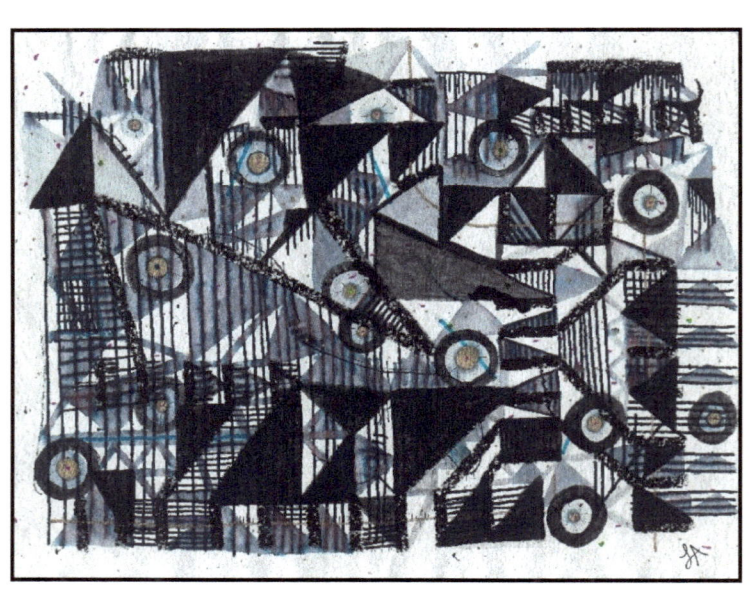

Circles & Triangles

Welcoming unfamiliar marks
Working with others,
Collaboration

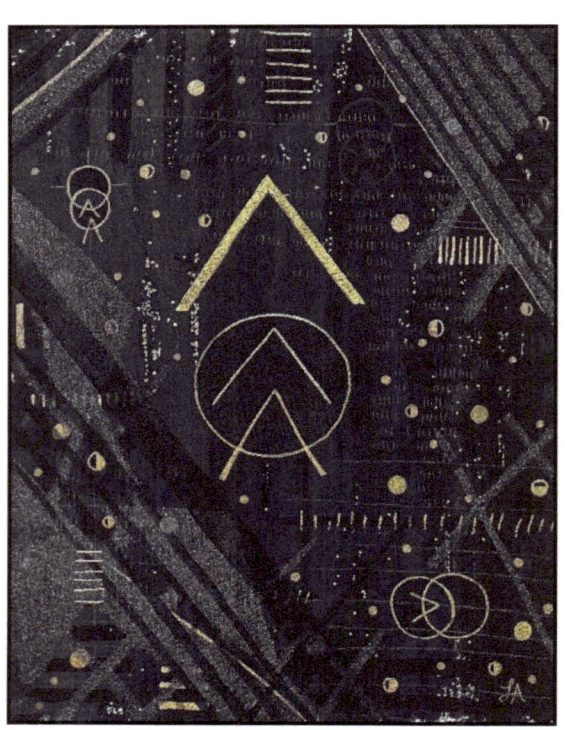

Direction

Layers upon layers
Up is the way to go

Evolve. The direction of progress.
Power, empowered, city, masculine, confidence,
dark as the night
Industrial Revolution
Invention, lights, power

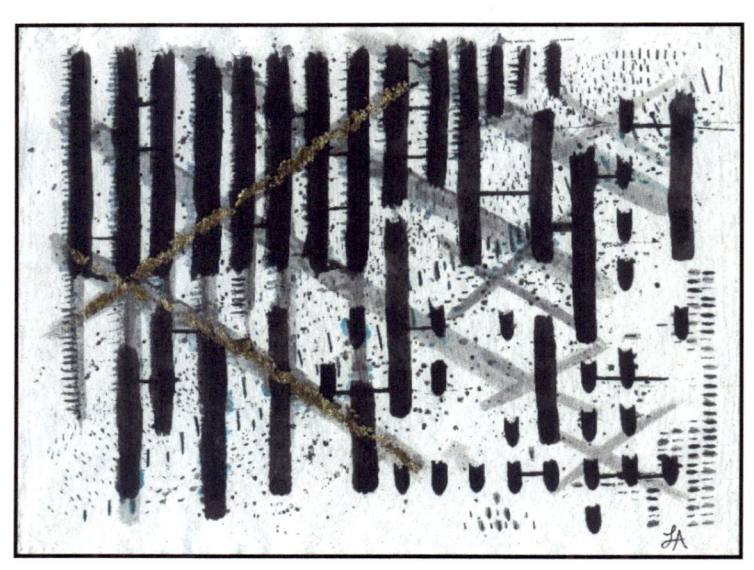

Golden Angle

Positivity, growth
Forward motion
an inclination
Confidence

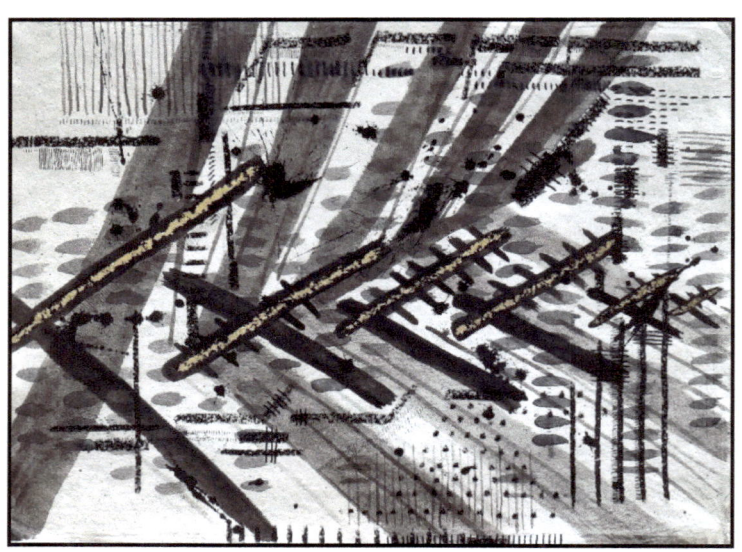

Golden Angles

Optimism
Growth
Expansion
Open-mindedness
Communication

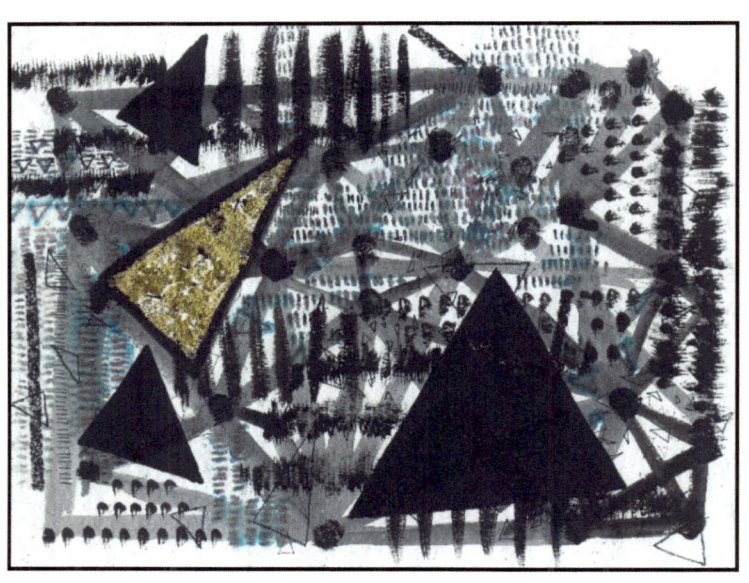

Golden Triangle

Hidden meanings
Hidden signs
Barthe & Sontag

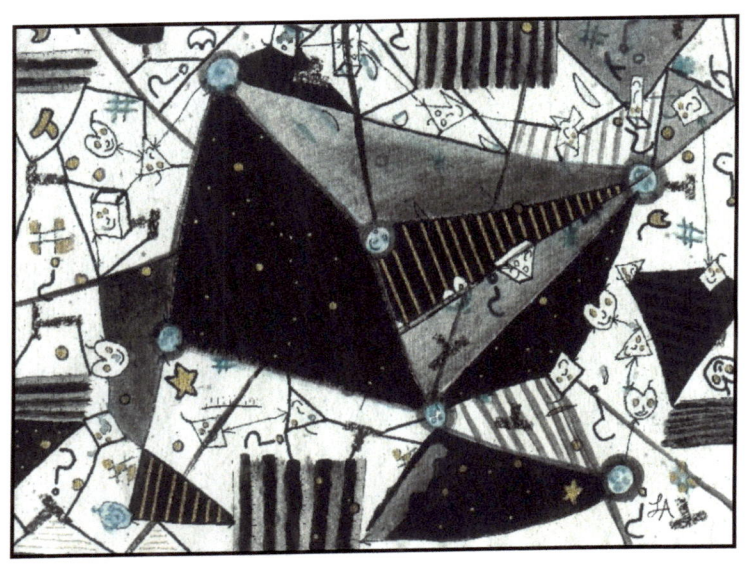

Happy

Shapes, smiles & fun

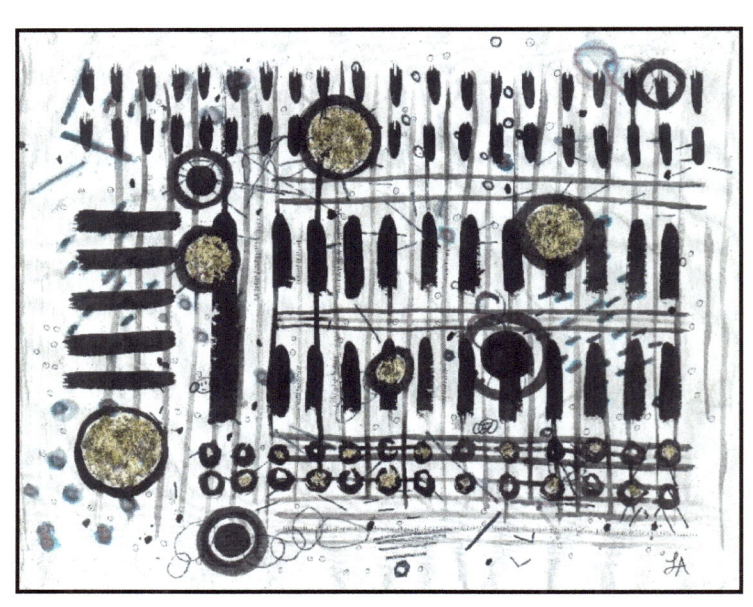

Notes & Keys

Letting Go
Intuition
Stories, language, visions
Rhythm of life

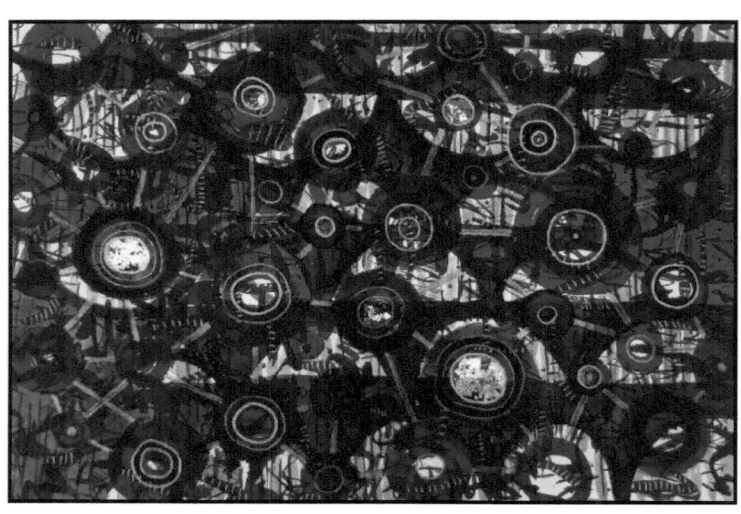

Wheels in Motion

Midnight Musings
Powerful encounters,
Transmissions
Throughout the night.

Artworks revealed
Spoken words
Thoughts in motion, thoughts stuck,
and thoughts thought-ing

Aligned

Discovering the essence
of your being
Deepest values
All Aligned

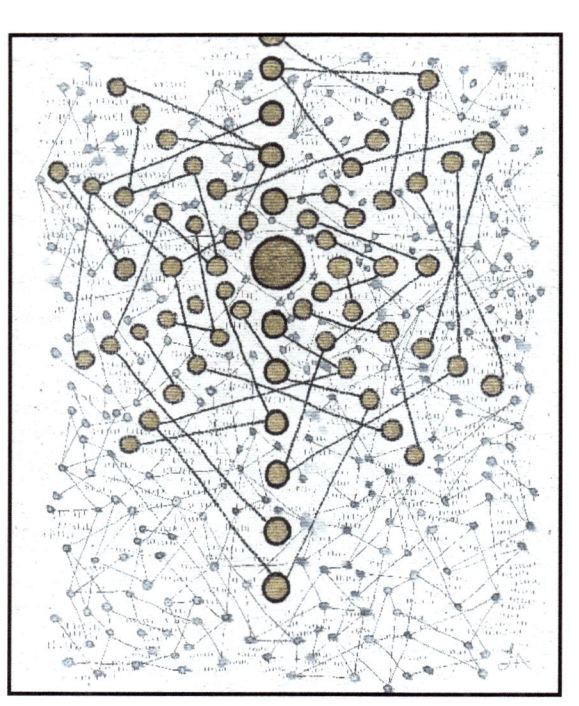

Chakra Web

Making sense of this large
Complex and intricate web

In harmony with something much larger than self.
Breakthroughs in all directions.

Angel number 133, 1:33 am, the
Vision came.
Happiness with where you are
and where you are going

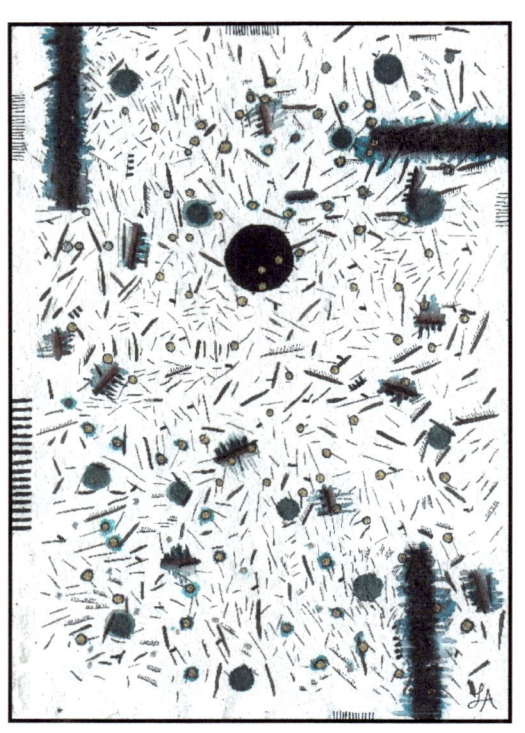

Confetti

Living in the present
Each moment
a gift

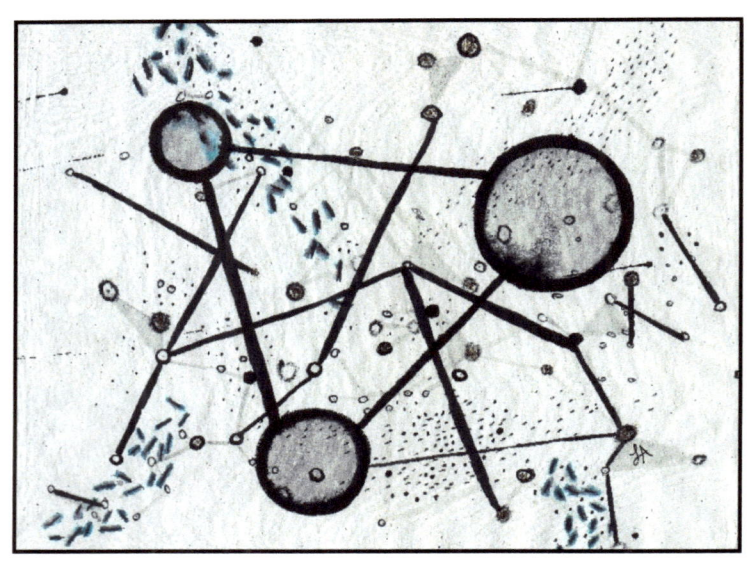

Cosmic Circles

Happiness, bliss, euphoria
The invisible force

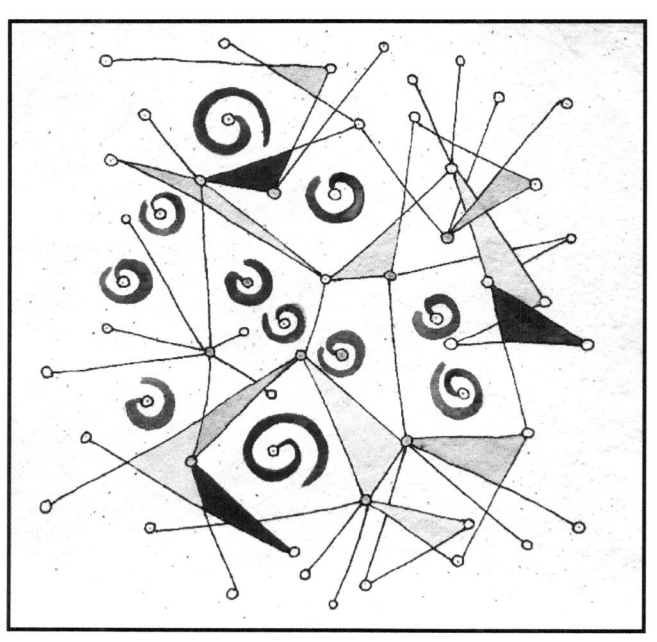

Spiraling in Control

Free from outside control
Not influenced or affected by others
Independent

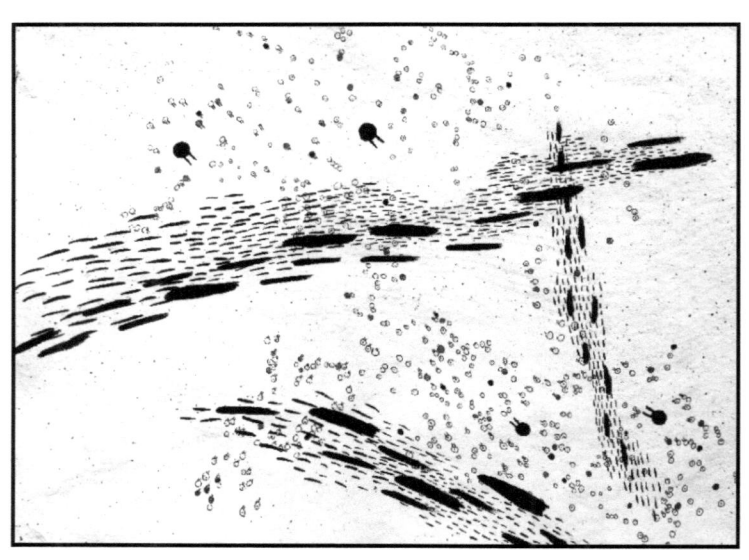

Jet Stream

Fuzzy lost
Get into the jet stream
Don't know where to go
Get into the jet stream

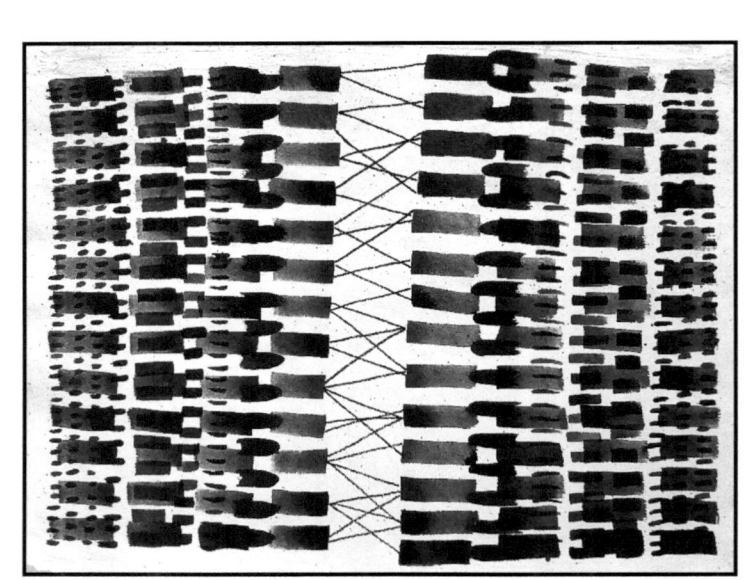

Synapses

Brain
Connections
Limbic, emotions, memory
Thoughts, planning, solving, attention

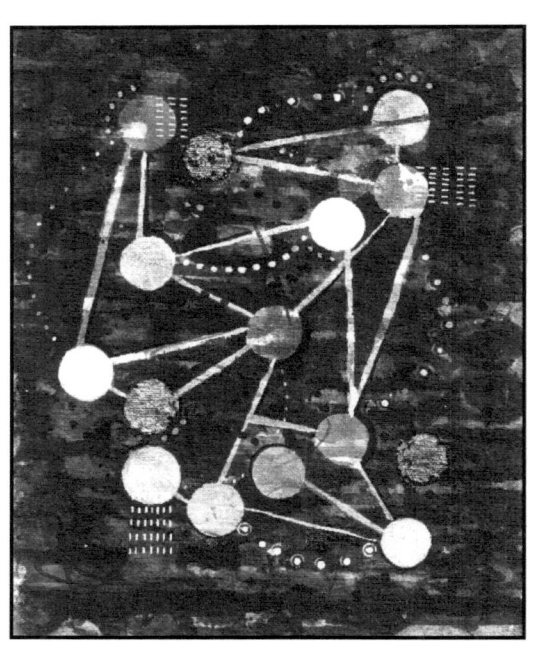

Phases

Dark times
Bright times

Road Signs

Breezes, Beeps, and Signs

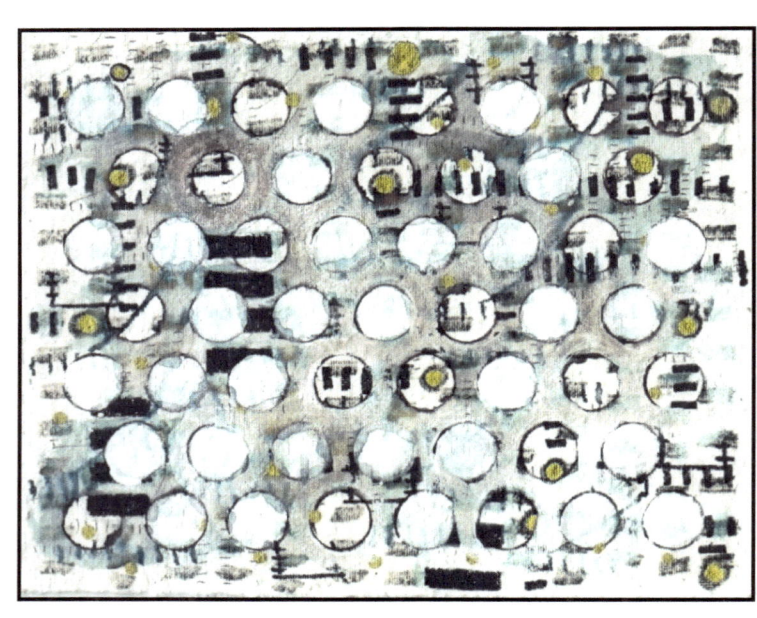

Glimmers of Light

Light Bright
Glimmers of hope

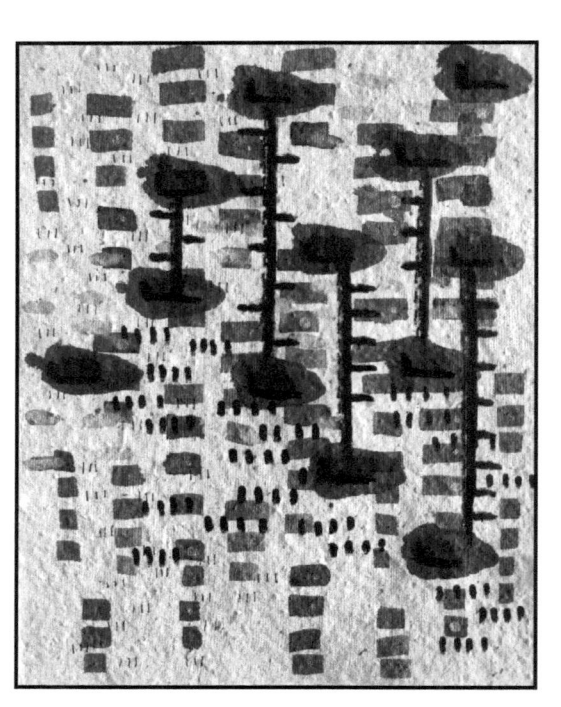

Celestial Ladders

Stepping
Climbing
Higher
Higher

Floating away from the daily dust

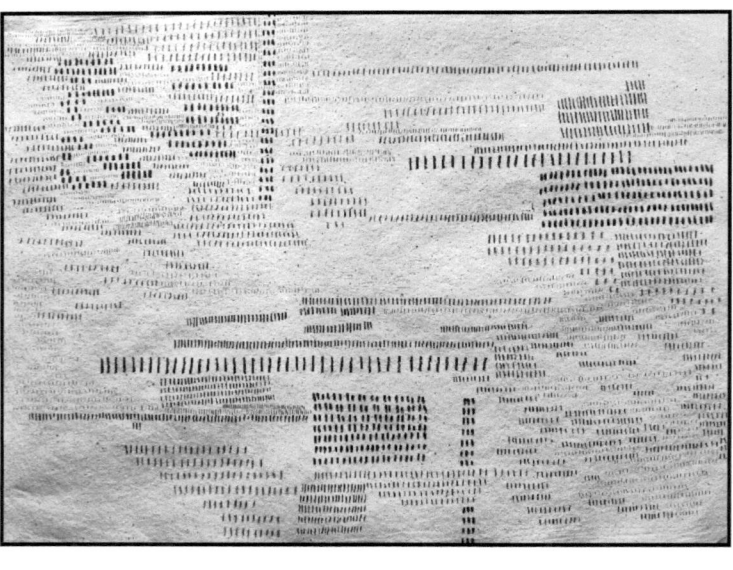

Marks for Their Lives: 3,113

It's More Than Numbers
The space between, the empty, the lost. The 1.5 million children, the Holocaust

Like computer coding, 1's & 0's
They repeat
Victims converted to numbers

Each line counted,
One by one
Each child gone
It's time for remembrance

Marks for Their Lives: 1,158

Waking up to 17,000 headstones
Too many, can't count
Treblinka's hidden graves
Symbolic cemeteries
Underestimated numbers, I lost count